HEALTHY BREAKFAST AND DINNERS FOR LOSE WEIGHT FAST

Description + Nutritional Table + Ingredients + Preparation and Much More ...

Eating well is not achieved only with salads but with a balanced and varied diet. It is important that the dishes are also attractive in terms of colors and smells (flavors, of course).

In addition, we must get out of our minds that dishes cannot have fat, there are good ones that they contribute to our body. Reduce the oil and use it preferably raw (cooking or dressing with a tablespoon of virgin olive oil is enough). Fish and nuts also have healthy fats.

Copyright Paul Williams

INDEX

HEALTHY BREAKFASTS AND DINNERS TO LOSE WEIGHT FAST _____ 4

TO START: SALAD WITH ORANGE, CHEESE AND PISTACHIOS _____ 6

SIMPLE AND HEALTHY SALAD WITH AVOCADO _____ 8

CUCUMBER CARPACCIO WITH SARDINES _____ 10

HEALTHY RECIPE: CREAM OF PEAS _____ 12

CARROT CREAM _____ 14

A VERY ORIGINAL HEALTHY RECIPE: CAULIFLOWER MASH _ 16

DO YOU LIKE PASTA? TRY THIS WITH AVOCADO AND BASIL 18

PASTA WITH HAM, ASPARAGUS AND ARTICHOKES _____ twenty

RICE SALAD _____ 22

SCRAMBLED EGGS WITH GREEN ASPARAGUS AND STRIPS OF HAM _____ 24

CHICKPEAS SALAD WITH TUNA _____ 26

SAUTEED CHICKEN WITH VEGETABLES AND ALMONDS ___ 28

SQUID WITH VEGETABLES _____ 30

MONKFISH WITH ALMOND SAUCE _____ 32

DO NOT GIVE UP ON A DESSERT THAT IMPROVES YOUR HEALTH _____ 3. 4

FRUIT MILLS _____ 36

HEALTHY BREAKFASTS AND DINNERS TO LOSE WEIGHT FAST

Eating well is possible. These healthy recipes prove it. Without too many complications and with ingredients that you surely have.

Every portion we eat should contain mostly vegetables and protein and carbohydrates. To make it easy for you to visualize it, without having to weigh, on a large flat plate (about 23 cm in diameter), half should be vegetables, and the other half, divided into two parts, one corresponds to carbohydrates and another to proteins.

- The proteins are in eggs, meat or fish, always in varieties that have the least fat possible. And do not combine them with each other. Choose only one. Proteins of vegetable origin (legumes) are a good option to combine with the first ones.

- Complex carbohydrates give you energy (cereals like bread, pasta, rice, couscous, quinoa ... or foods rich in starch like potatoes).

Avoid refined cereals, the integral option is better to provide fiber, which helps stimulate intestinal transit. And the best cooked or roasted potatoes (not fried, which are very caloric). Cut into sticks and baked, they are reminiscent of fried.

1.

TO START: SALAD WITH ORANGE, CHEESE AND PISTACHIOS

We started with some salads to continue with creams, dishes to improve health with eggs, pasta, meat, vegetables and fish. Ah! And we forget about desserts. This salad with orange, goat cheese and pistachios, these provide vitamin B1 and vitamin B6, riboflavin, vitamin E, vitamin K and folic acid. If you do not have, replace them with another dried fruit.

INGREDIENTS: 4 PEOPLE / 20 MIN

200 g of endive 50 g of arugula (substitute escarole and arugula for whatever lettuce you have) 2 oranges 300 g of goat cheese roll (reduce calories with fresh cheese) 50 g of pistachios 5 tablespoons of virgin olive oil 1 tablespoon of sherry vinegar Salt Chives (optional)

PREPARATION:

1. Chop, wash and dry the endive. Wash and dry the arugula. 2. Cut an orange and a half into wedges and remove the skin. Squeeze the remaining half to extract the juice. 3. Wash, dry and chop the chives. 4. Peel and chop the pistachios. 5. Prepare the vinaigrette by mixing four tablespoons of oil with the vinegar, two tablespoons of orange juice, a pinch of salt and two tablespoons of chopped chives. 6. Remove the crust from the goat cheese roll, cut the cheese into pieces, brush your hands with oil to form small balls and cover them with the chopped pistachios. 7. Distribute the ingredients on the plates and dress with the vinaigrette.

TWO.

SIMPLE AND HEALTHY SALAD WITH AVOCADO

Strawberries and avocados are the star ingredients of this dish that improves health because the former provide vitamin C, among others, and the latter are known as "green gold." Its potassium helps lower blood pressure.

INGREDIENTS: 4 PEOPLE / 35 MIN
1 bag of sprouts, 8 strawberries, 32 strawberries, 16 cherry tomatoes, 1 avocado, 1 date, 1/2 lemon, 1 orange, 1 tablespoon olive oil, 1 tablespoon poppy seeds, freshly ground black pepper.

PREPARATION:
1. Squeeze the orange and mix its juice, olive oil, seedless date and a pinch of freshly ground black pepper in the blender. Beat until smooth and add the poppy seeds last. 2. Peel the avocado, remove the bone and cut its pulp into cubes of about 2 cm. Drizzle them with lemon juice so they don't rust. 3. Cut the cherry tomatoes into halves and the strawberries into halves or quarters, depending on how large they are. 4. Assemble the dishes. Mentally divide the plate into 4 parts, as if it were the dial of a clock, and put the tender salad shoots in one, the tomatoes in another, the strawberries in another and the avocado in another. Decorate the salad with the strawberries and accompany it with the orange vinaigrette with poppy seeds.

3.

CUCUMBER CARPACCIO WITH SARDINES

A recipe for confinement that improves health and takes care of you because cucumber provides fiber, vitamins of group B, C, E and A and contains important minerals such as iron, calcium, phosphorus, magnesium and potassium.

INGREDIENTS: 4 PEOPLE / 35 MIN
2 cucumbers 12 sardines cleaned and sliced into fillets (you can use canned sardines) 75 g of goat cheese or feta 1 lemon Pepper For the vinaigrette: 6 tablespoons of olive oil 2 tablespoons of Sherry vinegar Capers 1 sprig of mint Salt

PREPARATION:
1. Wash the sardines, put them in a bowl and sprinkle them with the lemon juice. Cover them with plastic wrap and leave them to marinate in the fridge for 3 hours. You can opt for sardines or sardines in oil or preserved lemon. 2. Meanwhile, prepare the vinaigrette: beat the oil with the vinegar and a pinch of salt until you get a sauce. Add the minced mint and 2 tablespoons of capers. 3. Wash the cucumber, cut it into thin slices (with a knife and patience or with a mandolin) and place them on a plate, overlapping them. 4. Drain the sardines, chop them and add them. 5. Flavor with pepper, season with the vinaigrette and serve sprinkled with the cheese.

FOUR.

HEALTHY RECIPE: CREAM OF PEAS

The creams are perfect for winter and summer. You can take advantage of it to make healthy creams with the vegetables you have in the refrigerator. Peas are a source of vegetable protein and numerous minerals and prevent heart disease thanks to their cholesterol-lowering lutein content.

INGREDIENTS: 4 PEOPLE / 40 MINUTES 600g of peas 2 potatoes 2 leeks 30g of butter 100g of gorgonzola 2 slices of loaf bread 2 tablespoons of pine nuts 2 tablespoons of olive oil Parsley Salt and pepper

PREPARATION:
1. Peel the potatoes and cut them into slices. 2. Clean the leeks and cut them into discs. 3. Cut the bread into small cubes and toast it in the oven, 10 min at 180 ° (optional) 4. Toast the pine nuts in a skillet over low heat. 5. Heat the butter in a pot and add the leek. Cook over low heat for 10 min. Then add the potato and peas, cover with 1 liter of water, cover and cook for 20 min. 6. Season and blend. 7. Serve the cream very hot, accompanied by bread, pine nuts, diced gorgonzola and a drizzle of olive oil.

You can choose to use canned peas, just sautéing them but not boiling them in water. Accompany the cream only with a splash of oil and, if you have at home, some chia seeds.

5.

CARROT CREAM

Write this down: carrots are rich in vitamins (C, E, B3, B6, B1, B2); carotenes, retinol and folic acid. Would you like to prepare a cream with them?

INGREDIENTS: 4 PEOPLE / 20 MINUTES
1/2 kg of carrots1 onion2 oranges60 g of butter1 tablespoon of flour400 ml of chicken broth 100 ml of liquid cream50 g of grated Parmesan cheese20 g of pine nuts SaltPepper

PREPARATION:
1. Peel the onion and carrots, and chop them. Sauté the first one in the butter for 2 min. Add the carrot, sprinkle with the flour, pour in the broth, salt and pepper and cook for 10 min. 2. Chop the pine nuts and mix them with the cheese. Form the cheese crisps by melting 4 tablespoons of the mixture in a skillet. Make 8 crisp. This step is optional, skip it if you don't have ingredients or if you don't want to complicate. 3. Crush the vegetables, add the orange juice and cream to the carrot cream, adjust the salt and stir. 4. Divide the cream into 4 bowls and serve decorated with the crunchy cheese and pine nuts.

6.

A VERY ORIGINAL HEALTHY RECIPE: CAULIFLOWER MASH

Cauliflower (a vegetable in the broccoli, romanesco, cabbage or cabbage family) is healthy for its nutrients, which help reduce the risk of various diseases. They are low in calories.

INGREDIENTS: 4 PEOPLE / 20 MINUTES
2 potatoes 200 g cauliflower 70 g green beans 100 g smoked salmon 4 tablespoons Greek yogurt Dill, chopped 50 g butter 1 pinch of nutmeg Salt Pepper

PREPARATION:
1. Clean the cauliflower, wash it and separate it into twigs. 2. Peel the potatoes and chop them. Cook the potatoes and cauliflower in salted water for 15 min. Drain, mash and mix with the butter, dill, pepper and nutmeg. 3. Clean the beans, cut them and cook them in salted water for 12 min. Drain and mix with the puree. 4. Fill a pastry ring on a plate with the puree. Press lightly with the back of a spoon and carefully remove the ring.

You can add some shredded smoked salmon, even add some beaten yogurt if you like contrasting flavors.

7.

DO YOU LIKE PASTA? TRY THIS WITH AVOCADO AND BASIL

Pasta is healthy. It is not always accompanied by extra caloric sauces. Whole wheat pasta provides more fiber. We already know that avocado is one of the fashionable superfoods.

INGREDIENTS: 4 PEOPLE / 15 MINUTES

320 g whole grain macaroni 1 avocado 50 g black olives A handful of basil leaves 1/2 lemon 4 tablespoons olive oil 40 g Parmesan cheese Salt and pepper

PREPARATION:

1. Peel the avocado, cut it in half and remove the pit. Crush the pulp in the blender glass, together with the juice of half a lemon, 3 tablespoons of water, salt and pepper. 2. Prepare the basil oil. Wash a handful of basil leaves and mash them with the olive oil and a pinch of salt. 3. Cut the pitted olives into slices. 4. Remove shavings from the Parmesan cheese with the help of a peeler and set them aside. 5. Cook the pasta in plenty of salty water until it is al dente (respect the time indicated by the manufacturer). Drain well and arrange in a large bowl. 6. Add the avocado cream and stir for a few moments. 7. Divide this preparation among 4 flat plates, drizzle with the basil oil, add the olives and serve immediately, garnished with the Parmesan cheese shavings.

8.

PASTA WITH HAM, ASPARAGUS AND ARTICHOKES

Green asparagus have very few calories and provide a lot of fiber, also vitamins, especially A, B1, B2, B6, C and E; and minerals (magnesium, phosphorus, calcium and potassium). And artichokes contain phosphorus, iron, magnesium, calcium, potassium, and vitamins (B1, C, and niacin, a type of B vitamin).

INGREDIENTS: 4 PEOPLE / 55 MINUTES

Green asparagusShort pasta 1 lemonAlcachofas Serrano ham (you can substitute for cold turkey) AlmondsGarlicParsleySalt and oil

PREPARATION:

1. Clean, wash and cut 4 artichokes into wedges. Cook in salted water and lemon juice for 10 min. 2. Cook 350 g of pasta in salted water, until al dente. Drain. 3. Clean a bunch of asparagus, wash and sauté for 2 min in a saucepan of oil. 4. Mix the peeled and minced garlic with 20 g of almonds and the drained artichokes. 5. Season, add the pasta and serve with a few slices of ham and parsley.

9.

RICE SALAD

This recipe improves your health and you can make it during isolation to maintain a balanced diet. The two main categories are brown rice and white rice, but there are thousands of varieties among which you will be familiar with wild rice, red or basmati. The benefits of rice for your health are noticeable in the skin, intestines, blood, metabolism, energy levels, blood pressure, digestions or the immune system.

INGREDIENTS: 4 PEOPLE / 20 MINUTES
Rice to taste Spinach Olives Tomatoes Anchovies

PREPARATION:
1. Sauté an onion and garlic. 2. Add the rice, pour with the broth in the proportion that the chosen variety of rice needs and let it cook long enough. 3. Drain and serve. 4. Add olives, anchovies, spinach, and diced tomatoes. 5. Serve the salad cold, dressed with oil, salt and balsamic vinegar.

10.

SCRAMBLED EGGS WITH GREEN ASPARAGUS AND STRIPS OF HAM

The egg is a great source of vitamin B12 (cobalamin), concentrated mainly in the yolk. It also provides vitamin B1, B2, niacin, folic acid, vitamins A, D and E.

INGREDIENTS: 4 PEOPLE / 25 MINUTES

4 eggs 1 bunch of tender asparagus 1 clove of garlic 40 g of duck ham or Iberian ham (optional or substitute for cold cuts of turkey or ham) 2 tablespoons of olive oil Flowers Salt Pepper

PREPARATION:

1. Clean the asparagus by removing the hardest part of the stem. Chop up the biggest ones. 2. Peel the garlic and chop it 3. Heat the oil in a skillet and sauté the garlic and asparagus for 2 to 4 minutes depending on the thickness. 4. Crack the eggs into a bowl, salt them and beat them. 5. Add them to the pan with the asparagus and, over low heat, stir for a minute until set. Serve the scrambled eggs on plates and decorate with ham strips.

ELEVEN.

CHICKPEAS SALAD WITH TUNA

Legumes always bring benefits to your health. And canned they are perfect to consume without spending too much time cooking. Chickpeas are a source of B vitamins, above all, they provide folic acid and vitamin A and a little vitamin C. It also has many nucleic acids.

INGREDIENTS: 4 PEOPLE / 15 MINUTES
300 g of cooked chickpeas12 cherry tomatoes1 / 2 chives1 ear of cooked corn1 bag of lamb's lettuce1 can of tuna in olive oilOregano4 tablespoons of olive oilPepper2 tablespoons of sherry vinegarMostazaSalt

PREPARATION:
1. Clean the chives and chop. 2. Wash the tomatoes and cut them into wedges. 3. Toast the whole ear on the grill, turning it as it browns. Extract the grains with the help of a knife. 4. Rinse the chickpeas and mix with the corn, tomatoes, onion, washed lamb's lettuce and drained tuna. 5. Cover this mixture and let it rest in the refrigerator for about 30 min. 6. Meanwhile, make a vinaigrette: beat 1 teaspoon of mustard with the vinegar, salt, and pepper. Add the oil and a pinch of oregano and beat again until you get an emulsified sauce. 7. Serve the chickpea salad dressed with the vinaigrette.

12.

SAUTEED CHICKEN WITH VEGETABLES AND ALMONDS

This recipe is healthy and very appetizing in taste and color. In addition, the mixture of textures is pleasant to the palate. Adding nuts to dishes, such as almonds in this one, is an extra rich in fiber. The good thing about this dish is that you can use the vegetables that you already have at home.

INGREDIENTS: 4 PEOPLE / 35 MINUTES

400 g of chicken breast 100 g of carrots 150 g of green asparagus The juice of 1/2 lemon 150 g of green beans 1 zucchini Soy sauce 1 red onion 40 g of almonds A sprig of thyme 2 tablespoons of virgin olive oil 100 g of garlic garlic

PREPARATION:

1. Clean the asparagus and remove the base of its stem. 2. Peel the carrots, wash and cut into strips. 3. Top off the beans and clean the garlic. Chop the vegetables 4. Wash the zucchini and cut it into slices. 5. Peel the onion and divide it into feathers. 6. Cook the carrots in salted water for 5 min, the beans for 7 min and the asparagus for 3 min. 7. Sauté the chicken cut into strips in the oil, 3 min 8. Add the garlic, onion, almonds and zucchini and continue cooking for 2 min. 9. Add the carrots, beans and asparagus and cook for 2 min. 10. Pour in the lemon juice, 1 tablespoon of the soy sauce and the washed thyme, sauté for another 2 min and serve.

13.

SQUID WITH VEGETABLES

Take a look at the frozen fish you have and take advantage of it in this time of confinement. You can also order fish online and take advantage of it to benefit from the benefits it has. Squid specifically is a low-mercury food.

INGREDIENTS: 4 PEOPLE / 15 MINUTES
4 medium squid 2 carrots 1 zucchini 1 spring onion 1/2 green pepper 1 clove of garlic 1 sprig of parsley 3 tablespoons soy sauce 4 tablespoons olive oil Pepper Salt

PREPARATION:
1. Clean the vegetables and peel the carrots. Cut them into thin strips with a mandolin. 2. Peel the garlic and chop it 3. Sauté the vegetables in 2 tablespoons of oil, for 1 min, continuing to stir with a wooden spoon. Add the garlic and soy sauce, sauté everything together for a few more seconds, remove and set aside. 3. Clean the squid, wash and season them. Brown the squid in the remaining oil for 2 to 3 min on each side, until they are done on the inside. 4. Divide the vegetables among 4 plates, add the squid and serve immediately, sprinkled with the washed and chopped parsley.

14.

MONKFISH WITH ALMOND SAUCE

A recipe that improves health and takes care of you with fish, in this case monkfish, but that you can make with any variety of white fish you have at home. White fish is a source of omega 3 and receives this name from the whitish color of its meat. It is low in fat (less than 2%).

INGREDIENTS: 4 PEOPLE / 50 MINUTES
4 monkfish loins 5 tomatoes 1 head of garlic 2 slices of toast Salt and pepper 100 g of toasted almonds Parsley Virgin olive oil 2 tablespoons of red wine vinegar

PREPARATION:
1. Wash the tomatoes and put them on a baking sheet with the head of garlic. Bake at 200 °C for 30 min. Remove them and let them temper. 2. Wash the monkfish and pat dry. 3. Peel the almonds and reserve some 4. Wash the parsley, drain it and chop it finely. 5. Chop the bread and mix it with the vinegar. 6. Next, peel the tomatoes and garlic. Blend these with the bread mixture, the rest of the almonds, 5 tablespoons of oil, salt and pepper. 7. Brown the monkfish, on all sides, in 1 tablespoon of oil, 10 min. 8. Divide the almond sauce over 4 plates, add the fish and serve seasoned with salt, pepper, parsley and the reserved chopped almonds.

FIFTEEN.

DO NOT GIVE UP ON A DESSERT THAT IMPROVES YOUR HEALTH

Agave syrup or whole grain molasses are much healthier and sweeter than refined sugar and contain enzymes, minerals and vitamins. It is what we use in this recipe to sweeten: fresh cheese and kiwi millefeuille.

INGREDIENTS: 4 PEOPLE / 25 MINUTES
250 g of fresh cheese 4 kiwis 4 slices of filo pastry 4 tablespoons of agave syrup 60 g of butter or sunflower oil

PREPARATION:
1. Preheat the oven to 180°C. 2. Melt the butter over low heat and brush the filo pastry with the melted butter. If you prefer, reduce calories and saturated fat by using the same amount of sunflower oil. 3. Fold each sheet of filo dough over itself into a long, narrow strip, about two inches wide. 4. Cut each strip of filo dough into three equal portions to obtain three identical rectangles. 5. Prepare a cookie sheet with parchment paper. 6. Put the filo pastry on top and bake it for about 12 minutes, until it starts to brown. Remove from the oven and let it cool. 7. Cut the fresh cheese into small cubes of approximately 2 cm. 8. Peel the kiwis and cut them into slices about half a centimeter thick. 9. Assemble the millefeuille. Start by filling the layer of the filo pastry base with the fresh cheese and the kiwi. Then drizzle the mixture with a pinch of agave syrup. If you cannot find it, you can also use good quality honey or rice molasses or any other whole grain without added sugar. 10. Repeat for each layer of filo dough. 11. To serve the millefeuille, present it on a flat plate, decorate with a few threads of agave on top and serve immediately.

16.

FRUIT MILLS

A healthy and attractive way to eat fruit, which contributes so much to health. You will have fun preparing the millefeuille and everyone at home will have fruit during confinement. Take advantage of the fruits you have. There will always be a colorful plate with many vitamins.

INGREDIENTS: 4 PEOPLE / 15 MINUTES
8 yellow plums 3 skimmed yogurts 4 tablespoons of honey 40 g of peeled walnuts A sprig of rosemary 200 g of watermelon 200 g of melon2 red plums2 kiwis4 leaves of gelatin50 g of sugar2 sprigs of mint

PREPARATION:
1. Soak the gelatin in cold water, 10 min. Bring 300 ml of water with the sugar to a boil. Remove, add 1 sprig of washed mint, cover and let infuse 5 min. 2. Filter, add the drained gelatin and stir until dissolved. Leave in the fridge for 2 hours, until set; Stir it a bit 3. Cut the fruit. Make 4 large slices of watermelon with a pasta cutter and 4 smaller slices of cantaloupe. Wash the plums and remove the pit. Peel the kiwi. Cut both into thin slices. 4. Assemble the dessert alternating the fruit with the mint jelly and serve it decorated with some washed mint leaves.

Eating well is not achieved only with salads but with a balanced and varied diet. It is important that the dishes are also attractive in terms of colors and smells (flavors, of course).

In addition, we must get out of our minds that dishes cannot have fat, there are good ones that they contribute to our body. Reduce the oil and use it preferably raw (cooking or dressing with a tablespoon of virgin olive oil is enough). Fish and nuts also have healthy fats.

www.ingramcontent.com/pod-product-compliance
Lightning Source LLC
LaVergne TN
LVHW022307170225
803971LV00031B/708